Biograp] CW01501853

Dame Deborah

james

The Bowelbabe

Autor: Linda Jude

TABLE OF CONTENT

- Introduction **pg4-pg6**
- Deborah James Age, Nationality, Zodiac   Sign Ethnicity, Religion, and Many More. **Pg6-pg7**
- Deborah James Career **pg7**
- Deborah James Early Life and Education Qualification **pg7-pg9**
- Deborah James cancer diagnosis **pg10**
- Deborah James Height and Weight **pg9**
- Deborah James Net Worth and Income. **Pg10**
- Deborah James Social Media.   **Pg11**
- Lesser known facts about Deborah James pg11-pg13

- Deborah James (FAQ) — Frequently Asked Questions   **pg 13-pg16**
- Who is Deborah James?
- What is the age of Deborah James?
- Where does Deborah James Live
- Who is Deborah James's Husband?
- How did she die?

- Deborah james shared story. **Pg 16-26**

Introduction

Popular British author Deborah James worked for the BBC as a podcaster and host. Deborah James, who has battled cancer for years, writes a painful "goodbye" note as she and her family are being transferred to hospice care, adding, "Nobody knows how long I've got left." She later passed away on June 28, 2022. Deborah James's professional and personal lives are discussed in this article. Following the success of her BBC Podcast, Deborah James became very well-known online. As a result, many people started looking up information about Deborah

James online, including who she is, who her husband is, and how old she is. I'm here to provide you with all the information you need about Deborah James. James Deborah was born on October 1, 1981, in London, England, United Kingdom. Deborah James passed away at the age of 40. Continue reading this post if you want to learn a little bit more about Deborah James. Deborah James's wiki, recent news, age, height, weight, family, net worth, and social media will all be covered in this article.Deborah, also known as Bowelbabe, was an inspiration, and we are very proud of her for her dedication to philanthropic campaigning, fundraising, and her never-ending attempts to spread awareness of the cancer that affected so many people's lives.

In order to dispel stereotypes, combat taboos, change the way people talk about cancer, and promote awareness, Deborah shared her experience with the world. Her tenacity to raise funds and awareness was admirable, even during her most difficult times.

Deborah James Age, Nationality, Zodiac Sign, Ethnicity, Religion, and Many More.

Continue reading this article to learn more about Deborah James's religion, age, zodiac sign, ethnicity, and more. Deborah James was 40 years old when she passed away in June 2022.

She was born in England, and her zodiac sign is Libra. Deborah James is of Caucasian descent, and she practiced Christianity.

Deborah James Career

Deborah James wrote many books in her career such as F*** You Cancer: How to Face the Big C, Money from Nothing, How to Live When You Could Be Dead, and many others.

Deborah James Early Life and Education Qualification

Popular British author Deborah James worked for the BBC as a podcaster and host. Deborah

James, who has endured years of cancer treatment, sends a painful "goodbye" note as she and her family are being transferred to hospice care and state that "nobody knows how long I've got left." It is terribly sad to report Deborah James' passing yet she lives on in the hearts of her supporters. At the London School of Economics and Political Science, Deborah James taught anthropology and specialized in the study of South and Southern Africa.

Deborah James was 40 years old when she passed away. She was born on October 1st, 1981 in London, England, United Kingdom. Deborah James spent the majority of her time writing books and reading books because she had always aspired to be a writer and was engaged in both activities. Deborah James left behind her husband, two children, and parents. Deborah James has received numerous accolades for her writing. Deborah James' parents reared her and her siblings.

Height and weight of Deborah James

Deborah James's height was approx 5 feet 7 inches tall, which is in centimeters it's 170 cm and in meters, it's 1.70 m and had Brown hair and Black eyes, Deborah James's weight is approx 55 kg, in pounds which is 121 lbs and This is just an estimation made by watching Deborah James's pictures.

Deborah James Net Worth and Income

Deborah James was a well-known British novelist who also worked for the BBC as a podcaster and host. Her projected net worth in 2022 is over $1 million.

Debora James cancer diagnosis

Deborah James (@bowelbabe), who is only 35 years old, received a stage 3 colon cancer diagnosis in December 2016 that later progressed to stage 4.

Deborah James Social Media

Instagram @bowelbabe

Twitter @bowelbabe

Facebook Deborah James

TikTok Not Known

Lesser known facts about Deborah James

Deborah James's last name is Unknown.

College Deborah James — Unknown

Vancouver, Canada, is the place of Deborah James' birth.

The United Kingdom's capital city of London is where Deborah James was born.

Deborah James was born on October 1st, 1981.

Deborah James was 40 years old when she passed away.

Deborah James turns a year old on October 1.

Currently, Deborah James resides in London, England, in the United

Currently, Deborah James was a resident of London, England, in the United Kingdom.

Heather James is Deborah James's mother.

Alistair James is Deborah James' father.

Deborah James's sister's name is Sarah

Deborah James's Husband's name is Sebastien Bowen

Deborah James's son's and daughter's names are Hugo and Eloise

Deborah James (FAQ) - Frequently Asked Questions

1. Who is Deborah James?

Ans. Deborah James is a well-known British novelist, podcaster, and BBC host. Deborah James, who has endured years of cancer treatment, writes a painful "goodbye" note as she and her family are transferred to hospice care, stating that "nobody knows how long I've got left."

2. What was the age of Deborah James?

Ans. Deborah James died at the age of 40.

Deborah James was born on October 1st, 1981.

3. Where does Deborah James Live?

Ans. Deborah James was born in London, England, United Kingdom, and she currently resides there in a state of death.

4. Who is Deborah James's Husband?

Ans. Sebastien Bowen is the husband of Deborah James. Deborah James married Sebastien Bowen in July 2008. Hugo and Eloise are the names of the boy and daughter that Deborah James and Sebastien Bowen have as their offspring.

5. How did she die?

Dame Deborah James, 40, passed away after a five-year fight with stage 4 bowel cancer, according to her family.

She raised millions of pounds for research in her final weeks and was named a dame for her "tireless" efforts to raise public awareness of the disease.

Early in May, the host of the BBC podcast You, Me, and the Big C said that she had ceased undergoing active treatment and was receiving end-of-life care at her parents' house in Woking, with her husband Sebastien and their two children there. she died on 28 June 2022

Deborah james shared her story

In 2017, not long after being diagnosed with bowel cancer, Deborah told her story to the UK Bowel Cancer Center. Deborah was named a patron of their organisation in February 2021, and on May 12, 2022, she received a Damehood. She sadly died away on Tuesday, June 28, after openly discussing seeking end-of-life care. The article that follows was first released in August 2017

(in quote)

"It wasn't around 4 p.m. on a dull Tuesday when my life changed for me; rather, it was at 7 p.m. on a dull Thursday right before Christmas 2016.

"I am the textbook definition of a hypochondriac; I automatically assume that dizziness is caused by a brain tumor, a cough is caused by lung cancer, and blood in the stools is caused by colon cancer. However, years of CBT have taught me to rationalize every illness, including a recent change in bowel habits that I attributed to drinking too much wine, starting a new job, and the strain of trying to be a full-time working "super mom."

When I tell my GP that I believe I have bowel cancer during our routinely tense "question time," not once, but three times over the course of six months, I am actually laughed at. If only someone would have believed me sooner that I wasn't "crying wolf"! My blood tests and stool sample came back "normal," therefore everything must be fine, even though I was repeatedly told that I must have IBS, hemorrhoids, or worse case colitis.

"And still, I continued to lose weight, pass blood, go the equivalent of 100 times each day, and feel exhausted. I had a sixth sense that something was wrong with me because, for the first time ever, I was terrified of moving further with this.

"I'm happy I was able to take myself out privately to have a colonoscopy since I was tired of waiting for a referral. I was blind-sided at 7 p.m. on Thursday, December 15, 2016, when I refused the sedative and had researched what cancerous tumours would look like in a colonoscopy (total hypochondriac geek alert!). I stared my ugly 5.5 cm cancerous, ulcerated stage 3 tumour in the face and everything went silly. I made sure I went skiing, had finished the school term, and canceled three appointments because I was so afraid that this might change everything.

"On that lazy Thursday, though, I returned to the day ward in tears (perhaps from the gas and air!) and proclaimed that I know "he" found something since I saw it too. When the consultant inquires, "Is someone here with you?," something is wrong. The wonderful specialist enters calmly and confirms my worst suspicion. That although he can't be quite certain, he has discovered a sizable tumor that I will need to have surgically removed and that it's probably cancerous.

"When you are informed that you "may" have cancer, you experience a certain amount of incredulity. a sense that you are not the one who is experiencing this. You don't have time for cancer, I mean, "you" were out partying two days ago, ran five miles yesterday, run a school, and have to purchase Christmas presents! There was no plan for it!

"I wasn't sure what I had planned for my Friday night, but within an hour I was scheduled to return to the hospital the following day for a CT scan, an MRI, and a visit with the surgeon.

"My husband and I were numb as we left the hospital and began the strangest time and roller coaster of our lives. We requested the most expensive bottle in the store, a gorgeously rich Leoville Barton 1996, and then proceeded to drink it down as though the end of the world was imminent at 7 o'clock the following evening in classic "c'est la vie" fashion.

Second place was never an option for me because I've always been an overachiever, and I think my disease feels the same way. I would never develop a typical adenocarcinoma (the most common type of bowel tumour found). Oh no, I was going to develop a mucinous tumor, which accounts for 10% of cases of bowel cancer. In addition, it was going to have a BRAF mutation, which is extremely rare and difficult to treat due to its resistance to chemotherapy, aggressive nature, and lack of a "wonder" immunotherapy treatment. Brilliant!

Thus, four months after hearing the words "you have cancer," when I initially believed it to be a stage 3 and completely curable "hiccup" in my life, here I am, forced to confront the hard reality of being 35 and having to deal with stage 4 bowel cancer head-on.(unquote)

Deborah James has her own blog Bowelbabe, is a regular The Sun online columnist, presents the BBC podcast 'You, Me & the Big C', published her best-selling book 'F*** you cancer' and raises awareness on social media, TV and radio. Deborah plays a huge part in Never Too Young campaign, working with UK Bowel cancer center on issues affecting younger patients diagnosed with the disease. She's also a member of UK

Bowel cancer center Lay Review Panel helping to review the research that were fund and has raised tens of thousands of pounds for the charity.

James received a ton of fan mail despite the fact that no one knew her true address, showing that sharing the highs and lows of her life certainly had an impact on many.

'As I'm getting more and more sleepy and finding life a little harder, I've had more time to consider that I've never paused to realise the impact that our podcasting, and talking, and lobbying has had over 5 years,' James wrote in one Instagram post.

Small talk can actually save lives; it can have an impact that is felt for a very long time after it first occurs; it can also plant seeds that may never bear fruit. "Deborah james"

Following her death at the age of 40, Dame Deborah James was hailed as a "inspiration" by many who remembered her incredible life and work, including the Bowelbabe fund, which has raised more than £6 million for Cancer Research UK, and raising awareness of the signs of bowel cancer, which undoubtedly saved lives.

James, popularly known as Bowelbabe, passed away quietly while surrounded by family, according to a statement from her loved ones.

The broadcaster and activist, who was given the news of her bowel cancer in 2016, worked relentlessly to raise awareness of cancer, educate people about the symptoms, and combat the stigma.

She maintained her optimism and lived by the mantra "rebellious hope" despite undergoing numerous procedures, rounds of chemotherapy, and a recurrence of her cancer.

Printed in Great Britain
by Amazon

84128981R00016